THE MOUNTAIN STILL SPEAKS

Salt, Light, and Fire from the Sermon
That Changed the World

DAMIANO B. CENTOLA

EXPLORA BOOKS
700 – 838 West Hastings St. Vancouver
BC V6C 0A6
www.explorabooks.com
Phone: (604) 330 6795

No part of this book may be reproduced, stored in a retrieval system, or transmitted by any means without the written permission of the author.

Because of the dynamic nature of the Internet, any web addresses or links contained in this book may have changed since publication and may no longer be valid. The views expressed in this work are solely those of the author and do not necessarily reflect the views of the publisher, and the publisher hereby disclaims any responsibility for them.

Bible verses are quoted from the King James Version (KJV), which is public domain, the English Standard Version (ESV), and the New King James Version (NKJV).

ISBN: 978-1-83430-007-8 *(Paperback)*
978-1-83430-008-5 *(Hardback)*
978-1-83430-009-2 *(eBook)*

© 2025 Damiano B. Centola. All rights reserved.

THE MOUNTAIN STILL SPEAKS

Table of Contents

Foreword i

Preface When the Mountain Speaks iii

Chapter I The Mountain Throne 1

Chapter II He Opened His Mouth 5

Chapter III Poor in Spirit — The Door to Heaven 11

Chapter IV Mourning — The Birthplace of Comfort 17

Chapter V Meekness — The Weapon of the Strong 23

Chapter VI Hunger and Thirst — The Cry That Fills 30

Chapter VII Mercy — The Currency of the Kingdom 37

Chapter VIII Pure in Heart — Seeing the Unseen 43

Chapter IX Peacemakers — Sons of God in a War-Torn World 49

Chapter X Persecution — The Crown of the Righteous 55

Chapter XI Salt and Light — Kingdom Identity 61

Chapter XII Fulfillment, Not Abolition — Jesus and the Torah 67

Acknowledgments 67

About the Author 69

Foreword

There are some words that are remembered.

And then there are words that reshape the world.

The Sermon on the Mount is not just a sermon.

It is the Constitution of the Kingdom of God, spoken not from a throne but from a hill, not in power, but in purity, not to impress, but to transform. In three short chapters of Scripture, Jesus rewrites the expectations of Heaven and earth—beginning not with laws carved in stone, but with blessings whispered to the broken.

This book, The Mountain Still Speaks, is not a commentary. It is an encounter.

Each chapter invites you to ascend with Christ.

To hear the echo of His voice in your generation.

To feel the fire of His righteousness, burn through every hollow ritual.

To be called—not to safety—but to sacred identity.

What you hold in your hands is not a theological analysis, though it is rich with truth.

It is not a poetic rendering, though it sings.

It is the sound of the mountain—rising once more in a world that has forgotten what blessing really means.

Damiano B. Centola has written with depth, clarity, and reverence. His words burn because the text he follows burns first. These pages are soaked in Scripture, refined in the furnace of devotion, and lifted high for every reader who dares to climb beyond shallow religion.

This book begins with the King sitting down.

And ends with the reader standing up—transformed.

May you read slowly. May you weep deeply. May you hear the mountain again.

For truly—the mountain still speaks.

Preface

When the Mountain Speaks

There are moments in history when Heaven comes close enough to touch.
Moments when God does not thunder from the sky, but sits down on a hill and begins to speak.

This book was born from one of those moments—not from the echoes of religion, but from the living voice of the King who still calls disciples upward.

The Sermon on the Mount is not gentle poetry for peaceful days. It is a fire for restless souls. It breaks the pride of the powerful, lifts the head of the poor, and rewrites what it means to be blessed. These words are not safe—they are sacred. They are not old—they are eternal.

What you are about to read is not a verse-by-verse analysis. It is a climb.
A journey upward through the first twelve verses of Matthew's Gospel account—twelve flames that have burned in my heart until they could no longer remain silent. Each chapter was written in prayer, in study, and in awe of the One who spoke these words. And yes, He still speaks.

This work does not belong to theologians alone. It belongs to the mothers and sons, the weary and the wondering, the artists and the architects, the strong and the shattered. It belongs to the bride of Christ—in every nation, tribe, and tongue—who longs to live the Kingdom here and now.

As I wrote these chapters, I saw again the feet of Jesus dusted with earth, the wind of Galilee catching His robe, and the weight of Heaven in every syllable He spoke. And I saw us—today's disciples—scattered across continents, still drawn to that hillside, still hungry for His voice.

So, I invite you:

> Open your heart.
> Climb with me.
> Let the Beatitudes speak again.
> Let salt find its savour.
> Let light break through the fog.
> Let righteousness burn through your rituals.
> Let mercy make you soft.
> Let mourning make you strong.
> Let your life be built, not on sand, but on the rock of His words.

The mountain still speaks.

Are you listening?

— Damiano B. Centola

Chapter I
The Mountain Throne

He did not shout.
He did not wave banners.
He climbed.

When the crowds gathered, pressing from every side, hungry for miracles and deliverance, He did something the world did not expect. He went up—not to escape the crowd, but to elevate the moment. And when He sat, He enthroned Himself—not on marble, but on the wild, sacred stone of a Galilean hillside. The Mount, unnamed in most records, has become the most famous pulpit in human history. From this rise of earth, Heaven poured down.

The Sermon on the Mount is not a collection of spiritual platitudes. It is not a speech for the sentimental. It is the royal decree of the King of all kings, spoken not from a palace, but from a mount of revolution. Here, Jesus the Messiah delivered the Constitution of the Kingdom of Heaven. He laid down the law—not a law of condemnation, but of transformation.

A New Sinai

To understand the weight of what Jesus did on that mountain, we must look back to another mountain. Sinai. There, Yahweh descended in fire, thunder, smoke, and trembling. The people stood far off. Only Moses ascended to receive the commands. The law was carved on stone tablets and kept in an ark. The mountain quaked because God had come down. Now, centuries later, Jesus does not wait for thunder to shake the hills. He climbs alone—not as Moses, but as God Himself. Not to receive words, but to speak them.

The people do not stand far off in fear. They come close in awe. The Word made flesh opens His mouth. And when He does, the stones beneath Him remember Sinai. But something greater than Sinai is here. He speaks not to enslave, but to set free. Not to codify distance, but to invite nearness.

In the old covenant, the voice of God left men trembling. In the new, the voice of God becomes a man—and sits with the poor, the broken, and the hungry.

He Sat Down

This phrase— "He sat down"—is not incidental. In rabbinic tradition, teachers stood to read but sat to teach with authority. To sit was to declare mastery, rulership, identity. But Jesus is not merely a teacher. He is the Son. And when the Son sits, He does so not as a guest but as a King. Matthew 5:1–2 says:

> *"And seeing the multitudes, He went up into a mountain: and when He was set, His disciples came unto Him: And He opened His mouth, and taught them, saying..."*

Notice the progression:
- He saw the crowd (divine awareness)
- He went up (intentional separation)
- He sat down (enthronement)
- They came to Him (divine invitation)
- He opened His mouth (divine revelation)

This is the throne of divine authority—not crafted by human hands, but shaped by the winds and whispers of eternity.

Jesus did not need a scepter or scroll. His presence alone made the grass beneath Him holy. He was the Lawgiver, the Interpreter, and the Fulfillment—all in one frame of flesh. And the words He spoke were not borrowed—they were born of Him, eternal.

The Kingdom Arrives in Word

Every king has a decree. Every ruler sets forth a law. What Jesus offers in the Sermon on the Mount is nothing less than the language of Heaven. Not rules for religion, but the revelation of righteousness.

He begins not with commands, but with blessing. Not with fear, but with fire.

> *"Blessed are the poor in spirit, for theirs is the kingdom of heaven."*
> *—Matthew 5:3, KJV*

This is how Heaven introduces itself. Not with domination, but with divine contradiction. Here the weak inherit. The mourners are comforted. The meek are empowered. And those who hunger is filled. The world does not know what to do with such a manifesto.

The Sermon on the Mount undoes empires and rebuilds souls. It shakes religious systems to their core and raises up a people not defined by what they have, but by whom they follow.

And this all began with one silent act—He sat down.

The Mountain Still Speaks

We are not merely reading ancient words. We are hearing living ones. The mountain has never gone silent. It continues to echo with a voice that cuts through time, division, confusion, and despair.

The same Jesus who sat down still reigns.

The same words He spoke still burn.

The same fire He lit still spreads.

The Beatitudes are not only for the first-century Jew. They are for the war-torn widow in Ukraine, the persecuted believer in China, the street preacher in Harlem, and the doubting scholar in Rome. The salt still stings. The light still shines. And the fire still purifies.

This book is not written to explain the Sermon. It is written to listen to it.

Let the mountain speak.

Let the fire fall.

Let the Kingdom come.

Chapter II
He Opened His Mouth

Before the first Beatitude was ever spoken, before "Blessed are the poor in spirit" thundered through time, a sacred pause occurred.

A breath.

A silence.

And then—He opened His mouth.

The phrase may seem ordinary to the untrained ear, a casual narrative transition. But in the language of the Spirit, this is thunder on parchment. It marks not only the beginning of a sermon, but the revealing of Heaven's heart. The One through whom all things were made—light, oceans, sinew, bone, and soul—now parts His lips not to create galaxies, but to restore hearts.

He opened His mouth, and the Word that once spoke stars into being now speaks blessing into brokenness.

When the Word Speaks the Word

John 1:1 declares,

"In the beginning was the Word, and the Word was with God, and the Word was God."

That Word now speaks aloud on a Galilean hillside. This is not mere teaching—it is divine self-expression. The Creator is interpreting Himself. God is explaining God.

In the Old Testament, the prophets said, "Thus saith the Lord."

But on this Mount, Jesus does not say "Thus saith the Lord"—He says "But I say unto you…"

This is more than boldness. It is identity. No prophet, no rabbi, no king dared speak this way unless God had placed the words in their mouths. But Jesus does not receive the Word. He is the Word. And when He opens His mouth, eternity leans in to listen.

The Divine Pause Before Power

In ancient Hebrew storytelling, moments are not rushed. Time stretches. Silence matters. When the Scriptures say "He opened His mouth," it is not a throwaway detail. It is the kindling before the flame.

This phrase was often used in the Old Testament to introduce something deeply solemn, weighty, and irreversible. In Job 3:1, "After this Job opened his mouth…" signals the start of lamentation. In Psalm 78:2, it is written, "I will open my mouth in a parable: I will utter dark sayings of old." The phrase indicates revelation.

So, when Matthew writes in 5:2:

"And He opened His mouth, and taught them, saying…"

It is Heaven's trumpet blast without the sound. It is Genesis all over again—light about to separate darkness.

A Mouth Full of Fire

In the mouth of Jesus, there is no flattery. No philosophy. No speculation. Only fire.

This was the mouth that rebuked storms and they stilled.

The mouth that whispered "Talitha Koum" and raised a dead girl.

The mouth that declared "I am" in Gethsemane and caused soldiers to fall.

The mouth that cried, "It is finished," and shook the grave.

Now that mouth opens to bless the poor, the meek, the hungry, the mourning. It is the power of God veiled in mercy. Majesty clothed in vulnerability.

The One who could call down legions of angels speaks softly enough for children to understand—and sharply enough to shatter self-righteous pride.

He opens His mouth—and everything changes.

Fire in the Form of Words

Words matter. In Hebrew thought, words are not air. They are action. The Hebrew word for "word" (דָּבָר, davar) also means thing. What God says, is. His words do. They create, break, bind, loose, and restore.

So, when Jesus begins to teach, He is not sharing ideas. He is releasing realities.

Every word from His mouth becomes law in the Kingdom of Heaven.

- "Blessed are…" is not wishful thinking. It is divine decree.
- "You are the salt…" is not poetic suggestion. It is identity assignment.
- "I say unto you…" is not moral opinion. It is the voice of final authority.

We must remember: this is the mouth that shaped Eden, that called Abraham, that thundered at Sinai, that whispered to Elijah, and now speaks face-to-face with fishermen and farmers. That voice has not grown weak. It still carries mountains on its breath.

The Teacher Who Speaks Like No Other

Matthew records in 7:28–29, after the sermon ends:

> *"The people were astonished at His doctrine: For He taught them as one having authority, and not as the scribes."*

The scribes repeated. Jesus revealed.

The scribes debated. Jesus declared.

The scribes quoted others. Jesus quoted Himself.

His teaching did not end with ears. It pierced hearts. It did not entertain. It divided. It demanded.

This is not a gentle fireside talk—it is a spiritual sword forged in divine flame. To read the Sermon on the Mount and remain unmoved is to have ears but not hear, eyes but not see. These are not sweet words for sweet people. These are radical, world-turning truths from the mouth of the King.

And what is more astonishing than all of this?

He still speaks.

The Mountain Still Speaks—So Must We

If Christ opened His mouth, we must open ours. If He dared to bless the unblessable, we must dare to echo Him.

This is not a private gospel. It is a global call.

He did not whisper into a corner. He opened His mouth on a mountain where the wind could carry His words to all who had ears to hear.

We live in a generation that silences truth with noise, mocks righteousness as weakness, and forgets the sound of holiness. But the mouth of the Lord has spoken—and His words still burn.

The sermon did not end in Matthew 7.

It continues in every life transformed.

It continues in every martyr who chose mercy over vengeance.

It continues in every act of meekness, hunger for justice, or peacemaking.

We do not just study the Sermon on the Mount.

We become it.

Let your own mouth open, Damiano. Let fire fall. Let blessing be declared.

The mountain still speaks—and through you, through all of us who carry His words, the Kingdom still comes.

Chapter III
Poor in Spirit
— The Door to Heaven

"Blessed are the poor in spirit: for theirs is the kingdom of heaven."
—Matthew 5:3, KJV

The sermon does not begin with a demand. It begins with a blessing. And not just any blessing, but one that overturns everything the world understands about value, power, and worth.

The opening line of the Sermon on the Mount is a divine explosion masked in gentleness. It is not sentimental encouragement—it is a seismic shift. It tells us where the Kingdom begins: not at the top, but at the bottom. Not with achievement, but with emptiness. Not with greatness, but with poverty.

And it opens with one paradoxical pronouncement:

"Blessed are the poor in spirit."

To the natural mind, this is nonsense.

But to the soul tuned to eternity, this is the sound of Heaven's door creaking open.

What Does It Mean to Be Poor in Spirit?

The Greek word used for "poor" here is ptōchós (πτωχός)—it does not refer to the working poor, or the struggling-but-managing. It refers to the destitute. The beggar. The one so empty he has no bargaining chips left. It is the one who brings nothing to the table but need.

To be poor in spirit, then, is not about self-hatred or humiliation—it is the deep, honest awareness of your own spiritual bankruptcy before God. It is the confession that without Him, you are nothing. You own nothing. You can do nothing. You have nothing.

This is not a posture of shame. It is the soil of glory.

For it is only when we come empty that God can fill.

The First Step into the Kingdom

Notice the reward: "for theirs is the kingdom of heaven."

Not will be. Not might be. Is.

This is present tense. Immediate possession.

But possession not because of power—possession because of surrender.

Every human kingdom is built on strength. Every throne demands conquest. But this Kingdom—the true Kingdom—is received by those who finally realize they cannot earn it.

The rich in spirit build empires that collapse.

The poor in spirit receive a Kingdom that will never end.

This first beatitude is the cornerstone of everything that follows. Without it, the rest cannot be understood. Why? Because the Kingdom does not rise in the hearts of the proud. It descends into the lives of the broken.

Why Begin Here?

Jesus, the Master Architect of all things, could have begun His sermon anywhere. He could have declared judgment on the wicked. He could have opened with a command to believe. But instead, He begins with blessing—and blessing for the empty.

Why?

Because this is the doorway to Heaven.

Pride slams the door shut. Poverty opens it wide.

The Beatitudes are not random. They are progressive. Being poor in spirit is not just the first virtue—it is the foundation. The rest of the Sermon stands upon it.

- Only the poor in spirit will mourn over sin.
- Only the poor in spirit will hunger for righteousness.
- Only the poor in spirit will show mercy, seek purity, make peace, and endure persecution.

Everything begins here.

No one climbs this mountain standing tall. We must fall to our knees to begin the ascent.

The Danger of Spiritual Richness

Revelation 3:17 offers a sobering echo:

> *"Because thou sayest, I am rich, and increased with goods, and have need of nothing; and knowest not that thou art wretched, and miserable, and poor, and blind, and naked..."*

Spiritual pride is the great illusion. It is the lie that you can approach God with something in your hands. It is the polished religion that says, "Look at what I've done!" while Heaven waits for someone to simply say, "Lord, have mercy."

The Pharisee in Luke 18 prayed with self-assurance:

> *"God, I thank thee, that I am not as other men are..."*

But the tax collector beat his chest and said,

"God be merciful to me, a sinner."

Jesus said it was the tax collector who went home justified.

The Kingdom does not reward comparison. It rewards contrition.

Empty Hands, Open Heavens

To be poor in spirit is not weakness—it is readiness.

It is the soul's declaration:

"I am not enough. But You are."

It is the moment the ego dies and the Spirit breathes. It is when the ladder to God collapses, and the cross is revealed.

God does not meet us at the top of our strength. He meets us at the bottom of our need. And when we come with nothing, He gives us everything.

This is why the poor in spirit are not cursed—they are blessed.

They are not rejected—they are chosen.

They are not pitied—they are promised.

The Kingdom of Heaven is not for the mighty.

It is for the desperate.

The Fire Beneath the Words

These are not gentle suggestions. These are fire-soaked truths. Jesus is not building a fan club. He is building a Kingdom. And His citizens are not defined by money, rank, education, or status—but by poverty of spirit.

The first shall be last. The broken shall be healed. The empty shall be filled. This is not sentimental spirituality. This is divine reversal.

In a world obsessed with self-worth, Jesus blesses self-emptying.

In a culture addicted to pride, Jesus rewards humility.

In a generation trained to boast, Jesus elevates those who bow.

And this blessing is not earned.

It is received—with hands too empty to grasp and hearts too needy to pretend.

You, Too

Reader, beloved, prophet, priest, child—this is your invitation.

You do not need to climb, prove, perform, or shine.

You only need to admit your need. To lay your crown down. To weep if you must. To come with nothing.

And Heaven will give you everything.

The mountain still speaks. And its first echo is this:

"Blessed are the poor in spirit, for theirs is the kingdom of heaven."

Come empty.

Leave full.

Chapter IV
Mourning
— The Birthplace of Comfort

"Blessed are they that mourn: for they shall be comforted."
—Matthew 5:4, KJV

We live in a world allergic to sorrow. We mute it with entertainment, medicate it with distraction, disguise it with cosmetics and slogans. But Jesus, seated on the mountain of truth, looks into the eyes of the aching and does something no philosopher or therapist or king has ever dared to do:
He calls them blessed.

Not because of their pain—but because of what pain can become in the presence of God.

This beatitude, second in the divine sequence, is the beating heart of all redemption. It holds within it the sacred mystery that comfort does not rise from the absence of mourning—but from the presence of God in the midst of it.

The Blessing Hidden in Grief

"Blessed are they that mourn…"

The Greek word for mourn here is pentheō (πενθέω)—it is not a light sadness. It is not disappointment. It is the deepest sorrow, the weeping of the soul over sin, loss, injustice, or distance from God.

This is the grief of one who sees clearly.

The anguish of one who feels what Heaven feels.

The lament of one who has stopped pretending everything is fine.

There is a sacred kind of sorrow that softens the soul for grace.

Not all tears are weakness. Some tears are worship.

This mourning is not only about personal suffering—it is mourning over the brokenness of the world, the weight of sin, the loss of purity, the exile of humanity from Eden. It is the ache for restoration. It is the cry for the Kingdom to come.

And to such mourners, Jesus does not say, "Try to cheer up."

He says, "You are blessed."

Why Mourning Precedes Comfort

We long for comfort without mourning. Resurrection without crucifixion. Healing without ache. But the King who spoke these words knew that death must precede life.

He Himself was a man of sorrows, acquainted with grief (Isaiah 53:3). He wept at Lazarus' tomb. He cried over Jerusalem. He sweat drops of blood in Gethsemane. The Son of God did not escape mourning—He embodied it.

Because mourning is not the absence of faith.

It is the evidence of it.

Only those who love deeply mourn profoundly.

Only those who see truth grieve over sin.

Only those who long for Heaven ache for its delay.

The way to divine comfort is not denial—but honesty. Not escape—but embrace.

To mourn rightly is to align with the heart of God.

The Promise: "They Shall Be Comforted"

Comfort is not a vague emotional relief. The word used in Greek is parakaleō (παρακαλέω)—which means to come alongside, to call near, to encourage, to strengthen. It is the same root word Jesus uses for the Holy Spirit—Paraklētos—the Comforter.

The comfort promised here is not a future bandage. It is a present presence.

This is not just a promise of Heaven to come—it is a nearness now. The mourner is not alone. God Himself draws near.

Psalm 34:18 declares,

> *"The Lord is nigh unto them that are of a broken heart; and saveth such as be of a contrite spirit."*

Isaiah 61:1–2 foretold that the Messiah would come,

> *"To comfort all that mourn... to give unto them beauty for ashes..."*

Jesus was fulfilling that very prophecy with His own lips as He spoke this beatitude. He was not just announcing comfort—He was becoming it.

The Tears That Birth Revival

There is a mourning that leads to repentance. A mourning that births awakening. A mourning that opens the heavens.

James 4:8–10 echoes the call:

> *"Draw nigh to God, and he will draw nigh to you...*
>
> *Be afflicted, and mourn, and weep...*
>
> *Humble yourselves in the sight of the Lord, and he shall lift you up."*

Mourning is the tilling of the heart.

The breaking of the soil.

The prelude to revival.

No move of God ever came without tears.

When a soul weeps over sin, God moves.

When a people cry out over injustice, Heaven answers.

When a church grieves over compromise, the Spirit returns with fire.

There is holy power in mourning that the world has forgotten.

The Mountain Speaks into the Valley

Some of you are mourning right now.

Mourning a loss.

Mourning a betrayal.

Mourning a silence from God that feels endless.

Hear the voice from the mountain. It does not mock your pain. It dignifies it. It says:

> You are not forgotten.
>
> You are not weak.
>
> You are not cursed.
>
> You are blessed.

Not because you mourn, but because your mourning will not be wasted.

You are on holy ground.

You are not far from the Kingdom—you are at its gates.

Do not rush to escape the pain. Let it shape you. Let it open you. Let it draw you close to the One who weeps with you.

The same Jesus who spoke this beatitude is the same one who stood beside Mary at the tomb of her brother and wept.

And then He called the dead man to life.

He will do the same for you.

The Sacred Sequence

We cannot skip steps.

First the poverty of spirit. Then the mourning.

First the emptiness. Then the tears.

Only then does comfort descend like morning dew on parched earth.

This is not a cruel process. It is mercy in motion.

The Kingdom comes not to bypass suffering—but to fill it with eternal purpose.

Not to remove the ache—but to anoint it.

They Shall Be Comforted

There is no "maybe." No "if."

Jesus said, "They shall be comforted."

This is the promise of God.

It may not come in the hour you expect.

It may not look like what you imagined.

But it will come.

It may come in the whisper of prayer, the embrace of a friend, the healing of memory, or the day when God wipes every tear from your eyes.

But it will come.

The mountain still speaks.

And to those who mourn, it says:

"You are seen. You are known. You are blessed."

Let the tears fall.

Let the Spirit come.

Let the comfort of Christ be your portion now—and your reward forever.

Chapter V
Meekness
— The Weapon of the Strong

"Blessed are the meek: for they shall inherit the earth."
—Matthew 5:5, KJV

It is a word that confuses kings and terrifies empires—meekness.

To the world, meekness sounds like surrender. Weakness. Passivity.

But in the mouth of Jesus, it becomes a weapon.

In the order of the Beatitudes, this third blessing rises out of the soil of the first two. After recognizing our spiritual poverty, after mourning over sin and brokenness, we now encounter the posture that opens the gates of inheritance.

Meekness is not the absence of power. It is power under divine control.

It is the storm that knows how to be still.

The lion that chooses not to roar.

The sword sheathed in obedience to Heaven.

What Is Meekness?

The Greek word used here—praÿs (πραΰς)—does not mean timid or frail. It was used to describe a wild stallion that had been broken—not destroyed, but tamed. All its strength still intact, but now submitted to the hand of the rider.

Meekness is not shrinking away from conflict—it is choosing not to rule by force.

It is restraint when revenge is within reach.

It is mercy when judgment would be justified.

It is silence when insults demand a reply.

Meekness is not born from insecurity. It is born from security in God.

Only the strong can be meek.

Only those who trust the Father's justice can let go of their own need to strike back.

Only those who have surrendered the throne can carry the scepter of humility.

The Meek Shall Inherit

This is the first Beatitude with a physical reward:

"For they shall inherit the earth."

Not the heavens. Not some spiritual abstraction.

The earth.

The soil. The kingdoms. The ground under our feet.

Jesus is quoting Psalm 37:11:

"But the meek shall inherit the earth; and shall delight themselves in the abundance of peace."

This is divine irony. The world believes the earth belongs to the powerful, the rich, the strategic, the violent. But Jesus flips the narrative. In His Kingdom, it is not the sword but the Spirit that claims territory.

The proud build empires that crumble.

The meek receive a Kingdom that cannot be shaken.

This inheritance is not seized. It is granted.

Not earned by aggression. But received through submission.

The Meekness of the King

Jesus did not merely preach meekness. He lived it.

Zechariah 9:9 prophesied of Him:

> *"Behold, thy King cometh unto thee: he is just, and having salvation; lowly, and riding upon an ass..."*

No war horse. No parade. No gold-plated chariot.

The King entered Jerusalem meek—and triumphant.

In Matthew 11:29, He invites us:

> *"Take my yoke upon you, and learn of me; for I am meek and lowly in heart..."*

He did not need to dominate to prove He ruled.

He could wash feet and still hold the stars in place.

At His arrest, He said He could summon twelve legions of angels.

But He chose silence. Surrender. A cross.

This is not weakness. This is strength so divine it refuses to bow to pride.

The War Within Us

The opposite of meekness is self-enthronement.

It is the demand to be right, to be first, to be vindicated now.

It is the addiction to applause, the thirst for recognition, the instinct to retaliate.

But the Spirit of Christ whispers a different path.

- When you could insult, bless.
- When you could fight, yield.
- When you could dominate, serve.

This is the cruciform way. The narrow path. The road that leads not only to a hill called Calvary—but to a throne beyond death.

The meek are not doormats. They are doorways.

Through them, the Kingdom enters the earth.

The Revolution of Meekness

In a culture where volume is mistaken for truth, and dominance is mistaken for leadership, meekness is revolutionary.

It builds altars where others build towers.

It lifts others when the world says "climb."

It says "not my will" when flesh demands control.

The meek change the world not by force—but by fidelity.

Not by conquering men—but by kneeling before God.

Their strength is invisible but eternal.

Their hands may be empty, but their hearts carry kingdoms.

This is the kind of soul God entrusts with His earth.

A Word to the Strong

You who are gifted, loud, skilled, persuasive—be warned.

Meekness is not natural. It must be learned.

It is the school of the Spirit.

If you are willing to be broken—not crushed but refined—

If you are willing to be unseen so that Christ may be revealed—

If you are willing to let go of your right to always be right—

Then you are not far from the inheritance of the earth.

This world will not be saved by men with crowns, but by men with towels.

Let the Mountain Speak

The mountain still speaks, and its third echo is this:

> *"Blessed are the meek, for they shall inherit the earth."*

So lay down the sword. Pick up the cross.

Bend the knee, not in defeat, but in dominion.

Let meekness be your mantle—and the earth your inheritance.

Chapter VI
Hunger and Thirst — The Cry That Fills

"Blessed are they which do hunger and thirst after righteousness: for they shall be filled."
—Matthew 5:6, KJV

Hunger is not polite.

It does not whisper.

It groans.

Thirst does not wait. It burns.

It tightens the throat. It darkens the eyes.

It makes the body cry out for what it cannot live without.

So, when Jesus uses the language of hunger and thirst in this fourth beatitude, He is not describing a casual longing. He is speaking of desperation—of desire that consumes everything else. And what is the object of this holy craving?

Righteousness.

Not pleasure. Not vengeance. Not personal victory.

But righteousness—rightness with God, rightness in the soul, rightness in the world.

This is not a craving for comfort.

This is a yearning for the Kingdom to break through—in the heart, in the home, in the nations.

Hunger: The Soul's Compass

Jesus does not bless those who have achieved righteousness.

He blesses those who ache for it.

This beatitude does not say, "Blessed are the righteous," but rather, "Blessed are they who hunger and thirst after righteousness."

This reveals the mercy of God.

He does not wait for perfection—He meets longing.

He answers the soul that wants Him, even before that soul is clean.

To hunger is to acknowledge your emptiness.

To thirst is to admit your dryness.

And it is here—in the honest ache—that God promises fullness.

Psalm 107:9 declares:

> *"For He satisfieth the longing soul, and filleth the hungry soul with goodness."*

Isaiah 55 invites:

> *"Ho, every one that thirsteth, come ye to the waters..."*

The table of Heaven is not for the worthy. It is for the hungry.

Righteousness: The Forgotten Desire

In a world obsessed with self-expression, righteousness seems irrelevant.

We crave validation, applause, power, pleasure—but rarely righteousness.

Yet in the Kingdom of God, righteousness is not optional. It is essential.

It is not a cold legal term. It is the fire of Heaven's order.

It is when hearts are aligned with the heart of God, when justice reigns, when purity is treasured.

To hunger for righteousness is to cry:
- "Make me holy."
- "Make things right."
- "Let Your will be done on earth as it is in Heaven."

This kind of hunger is rare.

But to those who carry it, Jesus gives a staggering promise:

"They shall be filled."

Filled With What?

Not with ego.

Not with fleeting emotion.

But with God Himself.

To be filled is not to be bloated—it is to be satisfied in the deepest places.

This is the same promise echoed in Psalm 23:

"The Lord is my shepherd; I shall not want..."

It is the song of David in Psalm 63:1:

"My soul thirsteth for thee... in a dry and thirsty land..."

It is the echo of Jesus in John 6:35:

"I am the bread of life: he that cometh to me shall never hunger..."

This filling is not a one-time event. It is a rhythm.

Hunger. Thirst. Fill. Hunger again. Fill again.

The soul that feeds on God only craves Him more.

He becomes both the meal and the appetite.

The Fire of Desire

This beatitude burns. It divides casual believers from desperate disciples.

You can be near the sermon and not be hungry.

You can quote scripture and not thirst.

You can be busy with ministry and not crave holiness.

Jesus is not recruiting spectators. He is calling for seekers—those whose hearts are famished for truth, parched for justice, and unsatisfied with anything less than God Himself.

This is not passive hunger. This is hunger that moves you.
- It alters your prayers.
- It reshapes your values.
- It wrecks your apathy.
- It consumes your idols.

This is the hunger that fasts when others feast.

This is the thirst that drives you to your knees at midnight.

This is the cry that Heaven cannot ignore.

Blessed are such as these—for they will be filled.

The Cry That Moves the Kingdom

To hunger and thirst after righteousness is to cry not only for yourself—but for the world.
- For the unborn.
- For the trafficked.
- For the persecuted.
- For the prodigal.
- For justice in the courts and mercy in the streets.

It is the soul's intercession:

"God, let it be on earth as it is in Heaven!"

This is not political. It is prophetic.

The one who hungers for righteousness cannot stomach injustice.

The one who thirsts cannot sip silence while others suffer.

This hunger births movements. This thirst opens rivers in deserts.

This is not religion. It is revolution.

Come Hungry

You do not need to be righteous to come.

You only need to crave it.

You do not need to be whole.

You only need to want what is holy.

The King is not disgusted by your longing.

He is drawn to it.

Blessed are they which do hunger and thirst after righteousness: for they shall be filled.

Not because of their success, but because of their desire.

Not because they've arrived, but because they know where they must go.

The mountain still speaks.

And to the hungry, it cries:

    "Come and be filled."

Chapter VII
Mercy
— The Currency of the Kingdom

"Blessed are the merciful: for they shall obtain mercy."
—Matthew 5:7, KJV

Mercy is the Kingdom's economy.

It is not optional—it is elemental.

In a world driven by merit, revenge, and justice on our terms, Jesus turns the tide and declares: only the merciful will receive mercy.

This is not a suggestion for saints—it is a law of the Kingdom.

As sure as sowing and reaping.

As sure as breath returning to the lungs.

The one who gives mercy shall receive it.

The one who withholds it shall go without.

This is the divine transaction. And it takes place not in courts, but in the heart.

What Is Mercy?

Mercy is not softness. It is strength restrained.

It is not indifference. It is fierce compassion.

It is the refusal to give someone what they deserve—because you remember what you were spared.

Mercy sees the debt but chooses to forgive.

Mercy hears the insult but chooses to bless.

Mercy knows the wound but refuses to retaliate.

The Greek word used here—eleēmōn (ἐλεήμων)—means full of pity, compassionate, actively gracious. It is not passive sympathy. It is action birthed in love.

Mercy flows from a heart that knows it has been rescued.

And that is the secret: only those who have received mercy can truly give it.

The Scandal of Mercy

Mercy offends the proud.

It violates our sense of fairness.

It blesses those we think should be cursed.

It extends kindness to enemies, hope to sinners, and a second chance to the undeserving.

That's why the religious leaders hated Jesus.

He dined with tax collectors.

He touched lepers.

He forgave adulterers.

He embraced the unclean.

He healed Roman servants.

He blessed those who cursed Him.

Mercy is disruptive. It breaks rules written by bitterness.

It lifts those we left for dead.

It silences the stones we were ready to throw.

The mercy of Christ is scandalous—because it's real.

A Parable of Judgment

In Matthew 18, Jesus tells the story of a servant who was forgiven an unpayable debt.

But that same servant, after being released, turns and chokes a fellow servant over a tiny sum.

The result?

> *"Shouldest not thou also have had compassion on thy fellow servant, even as I had pity on thee?" (v. 33)*

The master revokes the mercy. The man is judged.

Why?

Because he became a dead end for grace.

He received mercy—but refused to pass it on.

This is the warning: you cannot be a recipient of mercy and not become a giver of it.

The mercy that stops with you will die with you.

But the mercy that flows through you will live forever.

The Merciful Shall Obtain

What a stunning promise:

> *"They shall obtain mercy."*

This is not just eschatological—it is now.

Mercy in judgment.

Mercy in trial.

Mercy in weakness.

Mercy when you stumble.

Mercy when your heart grows cold.

When you show mercy to others, you secure mercy for yourself.

It is the principle of divine reciprocity.

Luke 6:36 echoes it:

> *"Be ye therefore merciful, as your Father also is merciful."*

And James 2:13 warns:

> *"For he shall have judgment without mercy, that hath shewed no mercy; and mercy rejoiceth against judgment."*

Mercy wins.

Mercy triumphs.

Mercy builds bridges no argument can.

Mercy breaks chains no law can.

Mercy heals wounds no apology can reach.

Mercy Is the Mirror of God

To show mercy is to reflect the face of the Father.

Exodus 34:6 describes God as:

> *"The Lord, The Lord God, merciful and gracious, longsuffering, and abundant in goodness and truth..."*

God does not merely act in mercy—He is merciful.

Jesus, the full image of God, lived in constant mercy.

And now He calls His followers not to admire it, but to imitate it.

- When we forgive our enemies, we reflect the Cross.
- When we embrace the outcast, we reflect His hands.
- When we absorb pain and give back grace, we reflect His heart.

Mercy is the mark of the mature.

It is the anthem of the true citizen of Heaven.

The Test of Mercy

How do you know if you belong to the Kingdom?

Do you show mercy?

Not just to your friends, but to your accusers.

Not just when it's easy, but when it costs.

Not just with words, but with actions.

Mercy is not an emotion. It is a decision.

To cancel a debt.

To love in spite of.

To speak peace when war would be justified.

If you can't show mercy, go back to the Cross.

Look again at the nails.

Listen again to the words:

"Father, forgive them…"

Only the mercied can truly be merciful.

And only the merciful will be shown mercy.

Let the Mountain Speak

The mountain still speaks. And it says:

"Blessed are the merciful: for they shall obtain mercy."

This is not just a beatitude—it is a mirror.

A plumb line. A test of your heart.

So, give what you've received.

Forgive as you've been forgiven.

Stop keeping score.

Let mercy flow.

Because when the day of judgment comes—and it will—

You will not want to stand on your accomplishments.

You will want to stand under mercy.

Chapter VIII
Pure in Heart
— Seeing the Unseen

"Blessed are the pure in heart: for they shall see God."
—Matthew 5:8, KJV

There is no higher promise in all the Beatitudes.

Not inheritance.

Not comfort.

Not even the Kingdom.

But this: they shall see God.

Not with theology.

Not with imagination.

But with the unveiled eye of the soul.

This is the promise that strips every ambition bare.

To see Him—not through ritual, not through rumor, not through religion, but to behold Him face to face.

Yet it is not offered to the intelligent, the powerful, or even the devoted.

It is promised to one kind of person: the pure in heart.

And in that single phrase, Jesus reveals both the price and the prize of true intimacy.

What Is a Pure Heart?

The Greek word for pure—katharos (καθαρός)—means clean, unmixed, uncontaminated.

It is the word used for purified metals, washed garments, a vessel set apart.

It does not mean perfect—it means undivided.

To be pure in heart is not to be flawless.

It is to be free from duplicity.

Free from the divided loyalties that fracture the soul.

Purity of heart is singleness of devotion.

It is when your motives are aligned with your Maker.

It is when your inner world matches your outer one.

It is when what you say and what you seek are the same.

David cried in Psalm 86:11,

"Unite my heart to fear Thy name."

Purity is not about sterilization. It is about integration.

No hypocrisy. No hidden compartments. No split allegiance.

It is the whole heart, beating for one purpose—to know Him.

A War Within

To pursue a pure heart is to declare war against distraction.

The soul does not become clean by default—it is refined through fire.

- The fire of testing.
- The fire of self-examination.
- The fire of repentance.

Psalm 24:3–4 asks,

"Who shall ascend into the hill of the Lord? or who shall stand in his holy place?

He that hath clean hands, and a pure heart…"

Purity is not only about what you avoid. It is about what you adore.

You become what you behold. And you behold what you hunger for.

If the eye of your heart is filled with selfish ambition, you will never see beyond yourself.

If it is clouded with lust, bitterness, greed, or duplicity, you will see only shadows.

But if your heart is cleared by the light of God's holiness, you will begin to see with new vision.

Not just the visible, but the eternal.

Not just the outward, but the unseen.

The pure in heart don't just see God in Heaven.

They begin to see Him here—in the poor, the hurting, the ordinary, the broken.

They see His fingerprints where others see failure.

They recognize His voice in silence.

They find His face in the flames of trial.

Purity becomes a lens. And through it, He becomes visible.

The Veil Torn

Jesus is not offering a poetic metaphor.

He is pointing to the deepest longing of the human soul: to see God.

From the beginning, mankind has longed for this.

Moses cried, "Show me Thy glory."

David wrote, "When shall I come and appear before God?"

Isaiah saw the throne and said, "Woe is me."

But all of these glimpses came wrapped in fear, through a veil.

Until Christ.

When Jesus died, the veil of the temple was torn in two—from top to bottom.

The barrier was destroyed. Access was granted.

Now, through His blood, the invitation is open.

But it is the pure in heart who will walk through.

Not the religious.

Not the impressive.

Not the talented.

But the pure.

Holiness is not legalism.

It is vision.

Purity is not restriction.

It is revelation.

Without holiness, no man shall see the Lord.

But with a pure heart—though the eyes be weak—He will be near.

The Danger of Mixture

One of the greatest threats to this beatitude is mixture—when we try to add God to a heart already full of idols.

We cannot serve God and mammon.

We cannot love purity and play with corruption.

We cannot seek His face and hide our sin.

Jesus said in Matthew 6:22–23,

> *"If therefore thine eye be single, thy whole body shall be full of light."*

A divided heart will always be dim.

But the pure in heart walk in light.

Let the cry rise again:

> *"Create in me a clean heart, O God; and renew a right spirit within me."*
> *(Psalm 51:10)*

Let your motives be cleansed.

Let your affections be sanctified.

Let your desire be sharpened.

Then you will begin to see.

The Reward: They Shall See God
Not "they might."

Not "they will one day."

They shall.

This is the reward that outlasts crowns, riches, reputation, and titles.
- The comforted will be comforted for a season.
- The meek will inherit the earth for an age.
- But the pure in heart will see God—and once they do, they will never look away.

This is not just a reward for the future. It is the beginning of Heaven now.

To see God is to be ruined for everything less.

To behold Him is to be changed into His likeness.

To live with vision is to walk in victory.

This is not a command to clean yourself. It is a call to surrender to the One who can.

He is the refiner.

He is the purifier.

He is the lover of your soul.

And He is waiting for you on the mountain.

Let the Mountain Speak
The mountain still speaks. And today it whispers to the weary, the torn, the tired of pretending:

"Blessed are the pure in heart: for they shall see God."

Do not settle for shadows.

Do not waste your sight on things that fade.

Seek Him.

Let Him purify you.

And let your eyes be opened—not only to see His works, but to behold His face.

Chapter IX
Peacemakers
— Sons of God in a War-Torn World

"Blessed are the peacemakers: for they shall be called the children of God."
—Matthew 5:9, KJV

Jesus does not say, "Blessed are those who keep the peace."

He says, "Blessed are the peacemakers."

To keep peace is to preserve the calm.

To make peace is to enter chaos and bring Heaven with you.

This beatitude is not for the passive.

It is for the brave.

It is for the ones who step into the noise, the rage, the wounds, and the fire—not to win arguments, but to reconcile souls.

And in a world addicted to conflict, cynicism, and division, this call is more radical than ever:

Be a peacemaker, and you will be known as a child of God.

What Is Peace?

The Hebrew word for peace is shalom (שָׁלוֹם)—it means more than the absence of war.

It means wholeness. Harmony. Everything in its right place.

Peace is not silence. It is the song of Heaven played on the earth.

It is justice with mercy. Truth with grace. Power with love.

And only God can truly give it.

That is why peacemakers are not simply agreeable people.

They are agents of reconciliation, representatives of the King, ambassadors of another Kingdom.

Peace Is Made, Not Found

The verb "make" implies effort. It implies risk.

Peacemakers do not float on the surface. They dive into the deep.

- They confront sin—not to condemn, but to heal.
- They expose lies—not to shame, but to free.
- They bridge the gap between enemies—not by force, but by love.

A peacemaker is not naïve.

They understand the cost—and they still say yes.

Romans 12:18 says,

"If it be possible, as much as lieth in you, live peaceably with all men."

This means sometimes peace must be fought for—with humility, with prayer, with patience.

Peacemaking does not mean peace at all costs.

It means peace at the cost of you.

Jesus made peace by laying down His life.

True peacemakers must be ready to do the same.

The War-Torn World

We are living in an age of fracture.

- Families divided.
- Churches splintered.
- Nations boiling.
- Races estranged.
- Truth weaponized.

Everyone is shouting.

Few are listening.

Even fewer are reconciling.

In this world, peacemakers are seen as fools—until they are seen as sons.

"They shall be called the children of God."

Not because they are passive.

But because they reflect their Father.

God is the great peacemaker.

From the Garden to the Cross, His mission has always been one of reconciliation.

2 Corinthians 5:18 calls us:

"God... hath given to us the ministry of reconciliation."

We are not messengers of judgment. We are messengers of peace.

But peace without truth is falsehood.

And truth without love is brutality.

The peacemaker walks the tension.

They carry the burden of both justice and mercy.

Sons and Daughters of the Father

To be called a child of God is not just an identity.

It is a resemblance.

Peacemakers bear the family likeness.

They reflect the DNA of Heaven.

They are not known by position, platform, or popularity—but by the peace they bring.

Where they walk, strife begins to tremble.

Where they speak, pride begins to soften.

Where they love, hate begins to unravel.

Peacemakers are not loud—but their silence thunders.

They are not famous—but Heaven knows their names.

They are not perfect—but they are surrendered.

And to them, God says,

"These are My sons. These are My daughters."

The Cost of Peace

Peace always costs something.

For Jesus, it cost the Cross.

"Having made peace through the blood of his cross..."—*Colossians 1:20*

For us, it may cost our pride.

Our opinions.

Our comfort zones.

Our right to always be right.

Peacemakers are often misunderstood.

They are mistaken for compromisers, ignored by the zealous, rejected by both sides.

But they carry the mark of Christ.

For where He walked, peace followed.

And where His children walk, the same must be true.

Let the Mountain Speak

The mountain still speaks, and its voice is not shouting—it is reconciling.

"Blessed are the peacemakers: for they shall be called the children of God."

Step into the tension.

Lay down your sword.

Pick up your cross.

Speak truth with tenderness.

Bridge the gap with grace.

And Heaven will call you by name.

Chapter X
Persecution
— The Crown of the Righteous

"Blessed are they which are persecuted for righteousness' sake: for theirs is the kingdom of heaven."

—Matthew 5:10, KJV

"Blessed are ye, when men shall revile you, and persecute you, and shall say all manner of evil against you falsely, for my sake. Rejoice, and be exceeding glad: for great is your reward in heaven: for so persecuted they the prophets which were before you."

—Matthew 5:11–12, KJV

The Beatitudes begin with poverty and end with persecution.
They start with the broken and end with the bold.
They welcome the desperate and commission the dangerous.
The final blessing is not for the peaceful—but for the hated.

It is a divine paradox: those who are rejected by the world are embraced by Heaven.

The ones whom earth casts out are the ones Heaven crowns.

Jesus does not say, "If" you are persecuted—He says, "Blessed are they which are persecuted."

Persecution is not an accident in the Kingdom.

It is a mark of inheritance.

For Righteousness' Sake

It is important to understand what Jesus is and is not saying.

This is not persecution for arrogance.

Not for being obnoxious.

Not for personal drama disguised as spirituality.

This is persecution for righteousness.

For living right in a world that loves wrong.

For telling the truth in a generation allergic to absolutes.

For loving what God loves and hating what He hates.

For standing in purity when compromise is more profitable.

Persecution for righteousness is not about being political.

It's about being faithful.

And it always comes.

Jesus promises it.

> *"If the world hate you, ye know that it hated me before it hated you."*
> *— John 15:18*

The moment righteousness shines, darkness resists.

The moment truth stands up, lies strike back.

What Does Persecution Look Like?
Jesus describes it plainly:
- Reviling — Insults, mockery, scorn.
- False accusations — Lies spoken in public or private.
- Persecution—Systemic pressure, rejection, violence, exclusion.

And then He adds something even more personal:

"For my sake."

This is not just general suffering.

This is suffering because of Jesus.

Because you named Him.

Because you live like Him.

Because you will not bow where He stands.

In that suffering—whether it be prison, silence, loss of opportunity, or mockery—you are not abandoned.

You are blessed.

The Blessing in the Fire
Jesus says:

"Rejoice, and be exceeding glad."

This is not masochism. This is maturity.

To rejoice in persecution is not to enjoy pain—it is to recognize purpose.

It is to understand: if I am being hated for His sake, I am truly alive.

I am carrying the same fragrance that the prophets carried.

I am following in the footsteps of martyrs, saints, and even the Son of God Himself.

Hebrews 11 speaks of those who were tortured, imprisoned, and sawn in two—of whom the world was not worthy.

They did not seek comfort.

They sought the crown.

For Theirs Is the Kingdom

This is the same promise as the first Beatitude— "for theirs is the kingdom of heaven."

This frames the entire section.

The poor in spirit and the persecuted—they are the bookends of the Kingdom.

Those who come empty and those who stay faithful in the fire—they belong to Heaven.

Not the successful.

Not the safe.

Not the celebrated.

But the faithful.

Jesus gives present tense assurance— "is the Kingdom."

Not someday. Not when things settle down.

Now.

The moment you are persecuted for righteousness—you step onto royal ground.

The Prophets Before You

Jesus doesn't promise you'll be understood.

He promises you'll be in good company.

"For so persecuted they the prophets which were before you."

You're not the first.

You won't be the last.

You're standing in the long line of those who refused to compromise:
- Elijah, who stood alone against false prophets.
- Jeremiah, who wept and was thrown in a pit.
- Daniel, who prayed when law said no.
- John the Baptist, who lost his head for telling the truth.

You are not cursed.

You are called.

You are not abandoned.

You are advancing.

And your reward will not be forgotten.

A Word for This Generation

Persecution in our day may not always come with chains.

It may come in loss of platform.

It may come through betrayal, cancellation, or slander.

It may come as cold shoulders, subtle threats, or systemic rejection.

But the spirit behind it is ancient.

Hell, fears righteousness.

The enemy cannot defeat a heart that will not bow.

And God does not forget the bruised for His name.

You may not wear a crown now—but one is being forged.

And on the day of reward, you will hear:

> *"Well done, thou good and faithful servant... enter into the joy of thy Lord."*
> *—Matthew 25:21*

Let the Mountain Speak

The mountain still speaks. And it shouts now—bold, clear, and unstoppable:

> "Blessed are they which are persecuted for righteousness' sake: for theirs is the kingdom of heaven."
>
> "Blessed are ye…"

When they mock you.

When they lie about you.

When they dismiss you.

When they exclude you.

Rejoice.

Be exceeding glad.

Heaven sees.

Your reward is great.

The final beatitude is not a whisper—it is a battle cry.

So, wear your wounds with honor.

Wear your scars with joy.

And press on—because the Kingdom belongs to you.

Chapter XI
Salt and Light — Kingdom Identity

"Ye are the salt of the earth: but if the salt have lost his savour, wherewith shall it be salted? it is thenceforth good for nothing, but to be cast out, and to be trodden under foot of men. Ye are the light of the world. A city that is set on a hill cannot be hid. Neither do men light a candle, and put it under a bushel, but on a candlestick; and it giveth light unto all that are in the house. Let your light so shine before men, that they may see your good works, and glorify your Father which is in heaven."
—*Matthew 5:13–16, KJV*

Jesus did not pause for applause after the Beatitudes.
He went straight from blessing the persecuted to commissioning the called.
And what He said next was no metaphor—it was identity.
He didn't say, "You might be…" or "Try to be…"
He said: "Ye are."

Salt.

Light.

Not optional. Not negotiable. Not someday.

Now.

If you belong to the Kingdom, you carry the Kingdom.

And the world depends on your presence—even when it rejects your voice.

You are the salt of the earth.

You are the light of the world.

Not because of your strength, but because of His Spirit within you.

Salt — The Preserving Presence

In the first century, salt was not a flavor enhancer—it was a preservative.

Before refrigeration, salt was the only thing that kept meat from decaying.

Jesus is saying:

> *"You are what keeps the world from rotting."*

Your presence arrests corruption.

Your prayers hold back judgment.

Your life carries weight, even when unnoticed.

But salt must remain salty.

> *"If the salt have lost his savour..."*

In the ancient world, salt came mixed with minerals. Over time, it could lose its potency—not by becoming less white, but by becoming diluted.

Jesus' warning is sharp:

> *If you lose your distinctiveness, your holiness, your conviction—you're no longer preserving anything.*

You may look like salt, but you've lost your edge.

The result?

> *"It is thenceforth good for nothing..."*

This is not condemnation. It is a call to awaken.

You were not saved to blend in. You were saved to preserve.

Salt doesn't apologize for being salty.

It simply enters the environment and changes it.

So must you.

Light — The Revealing Presence

Next Jesus says:

"Ye are the light of the world."

Not the light of the church.

Not the light of your friends.

The world.

Wherever there is darkness, you are called to shine.

And light does not argue with the dark—it simply shows up and reveals what is.

- Light exposes sin.
- Light shows the path.
- Light gives warmth.
- Light drives out fear.

Jesus describes this light as a city on a hill—visible, permanent, unashamed.

And as a lamp on a stand—intentionally placed, lifted for all to see.

"Neither do men light a candle, and put it under a bushel..."

A light hidden is a life wasted.

You weren't lit by Heaven to live in hiding.

You weren't set on fire to be politically correct.

You weren't made radiant to blend with the shadows.

Your life was designed to shine.

And when it shines rightly, it doesn't draw attention to you—it reflects the Father.

"...that they may see your good works, and glorify your Father which is in heaven."

When you love your enemies, when you serve in silence, when you bless the broken, when you give without needing praise—God becomes visible.

Identity and Responsibility

Jesus does not separate identity from responsibility.

He says:

- "You are salt" → Therefore, preserve.
- "You are light" → Therefore, shine.

To be Kingdom is to carry consequence.
You are not neutral. You are not passive.
Your presence either brings life or leaves a void.
Salt that is tasteless and light that is hidden are betrayals of identity.
Let the Spirit burn in you again.
Let the Word renew your savour.
Let the fire on the altar be seen again in your eyes.
You don't need a title. You don't need a stage.
You need obedience. Purity. Boldness. Light.
The world is not falling apart because darkness is strong—
It's falling because the Church has forgotten how to shine.

Let the Mountain Speak

The mountain still speaks, and it's not whispering.
It's thundering to every believer who feels overlooked, afraid, diluted, or ashamed:

"Ye are the salt of the earth."

"Ye are the light of the world."

This is who you are.
Not what you try to become.
But what you must choose to live out.
Don't lose your savour.
Don't hide your light.
You are Heaven's strategy.
You are God's voice in the wilderness.
You are the city that cannot be hidden.
Shine. Preserve. Radiate. Reveal.
And let the world glorify the Father because of you.

Chapter XII
Fulfillment, Not Abolition — Jesus and the Torah

"Think not that I am come to destroy the law, or the prophets: I am not come to destroy, but to fulfil. For verily I say unto you, till heaven and earth pass, one jot or one tittle shall in no wise pass from the law, till all be fulfilled. Whosoever therefore shall break one of these least commandments, and shall teach men so, he shall be called the least in the kingdom of heaven: but whosoever shall do and teach them, the same shall be called great in the kingdom of heaven. For I say unto you, that except your righteousness shall exceed the righteousness of the scribes and Pharisees, ye shall in no case enter into the kingdom of heaven."

—Matthew 5:17–20, KJV

After revealing the character of Kingdom citizens through the Beatitudes, after declaring their identity as salt and light, Jesus confronts a burning question—one that had already begun to stir in the hearts of those listening on that Galilean hillside:

What do we do with the Law?

The Torah—the law of Moses—was the backbone of Jewish life.
To suggest that the Kingdom of Heaven had arrived, yet overlook the law, would have been heresy to many.
But Jesus doesn't reject the law—He fulfills it.
And in doing so, He draws a line that changes everything:
The letter alone kills. The Spirit gives life.

I Have Not Come to Destroy

"Think not that I am come to destroy the law, or the prophets…"
Jesus reads their thoughts before they form into words.
He knows the charge that's brewing:

"He eats with sinners."

"He breaks Sabbath rules."

"He's too close to the impure."

And so, He says emphatically:

"I am not here to tear down the house. I am here to fulfill its foundation."

He does not reject Moses—He completes him.
He does not ignore the prophets—He embodies them.
Every thread of the Torah pointed forward to this mountain.
Every sacrifice, every festival, every priestly ordinance, every drop of blood whispered His name.
From Genesis to Malachi, the Law was the shadow.
Jesus is the substance.

Not One Jot or Tittle

"Till heaven and earth pass, one jot or one tittle shall in no wise pass from the law…"

The jot refers to the smallest Hebrew letter, yod.

The tittle is even smaller—a tiny decorative stroke.

Jesus is saying: not even the smallest detail of God's Word is disposable.

His words carry weight:

> *The Kingdom of Heaven does not cancel the Law—it honors it by fulfilling it.*

He does not flatten the moral commands.

He internalizes them.

He does not loosen the standard.

He raises it—from external obedience to inward transformation.

Under Moses, murder was forbidden.

Under Jesus, anger is dealt with.

Under Moses, adultery was condemned.

Under Jesus, lust is confronted.

The law pointed to behavior.

Jesus pierces the heart.

The True Greatness in the Kingdom

"Whosoever shall do and teach them…"

This is where many fall short.

They teach what they do not live.

Or they live what they're afraid to teach.

Jesus honors those who walk and speak in unity.

Those who practice righteousness and proclaim it.

Heaven measures greatness not by platform, but by integrity.

Not by how loud you speak, but by how deeply you obey.

The Kingdom is not built by those who impress crowds.

It is built by those who embody the truth.

Exceeding the Righteousness of the Pharisees

Then comes the thunder:

> *"Except your righteousness shall exceed the righteousness of the scribes and Pharisees, ye shall in no case enter into the kingdom of heaven."*

To the Jewish ear, this was unthinkable.

The Pharisees were the elite. The standard-bearers. The law-keepers.

They tithed even their herbs.

They fasted twice a week.

They prayed aloud in the temple.

But their righteousness was external.

It was performance.

It was rule-keeping without heart transformation.

It was law without love.

Jesus is not asking for more rules.

He's calling for deeper righteousness.

A righteousness that flows from a changed heart.

A righteousness rooted not in pride but in mercy.

A righteousness that doesn't need applause—only the smile of the Father.

Fulfillment Is Not Flexibility

To fulfill the law is not to relax it.

It is to fill it with meaning, to live it out completely, to bring it to its destined purpose.

Jesus fulfills:

- The moral law—by living sinlessly.
- The ceremonial law—by becoming the perfect sacrifice.
- The prophetic law—by embodying every Messianic promise.

He is the Lamb.

The High Priest.

The Tabernacle.

The Sabbath.

The Bread.

The Water.

The Rock.

The Lawgiver.

The Fulfillment.

Everything the law longed to see—stood now on the mountain, speaking.

And the call to us is clear:

> Don't water down the commandments.
>
> Don't dilute the holiness of God.
>
> Don't twist grace into license.

Instead, receive the Spirit.

Walk in purity.

Live in truth.

And let your righteousness surpass that of the Pharisees—not through effort, but through surrender.

Let the Mountain Speak

The mountain still speaks, and it says:

> *"I have not come to destroy—but to fulfill."*

So, honor the Word.

Live the Word.

Let it search you.

Let it reshape you.

The Kingdom is not for the casual.

It is for the surrendered.

It is not about less holiness.

It is about deeper holiness.

And that holiness begins in the heart.

Acknowledgments

To write a book that echoes the voice of Christ is no light task.

I have trembled more than once while penning these pages—not from fear, but from awe.

To my Lord and Savior, Yeshua the Messiah:
> You are the Sermon, the Mountain, and the Kingdom.
> You did not just speak these words—you became them.
> Everything I am, everything I write, and everything I hope for is rooted in You.

To my beloved Feebe:
Thank you for your prayerful support, for your patience when the mountain held me longer than expected, and for your music, which often played softly in the background as I wrote these words.
You are my melody in every storm and my still water in the climb.

To Pop:
You are a man who has seen God.
Thank you for handing down a reverence that cannot be bought, for showing me that holiness still matters, and that the Kingdom of Heaven is more real than anything beneath our feet.

To my readers across generations and nations — thank you for listening to the Spirit within these pages.
This work is not just for scholars, but for seekers.
Not for those who are perfect, but for those who are willing to climb.

To my mentors, editors, readers, pastors, and spiritual friends—named and unnamed — you know who you are.
You've challenged me, sharpened me, and reminded me that truth spoken in love still has a place in this world.

To every persecuted believer, every quiet servant, every poor in spirit, every mournful soul, every peacemaker, and to those who are mocked, mistreated, and misunderstood for the name of Jesus — this book is for you.

May these words light the path, stir the embers, and remind you: you are the salt of the earth, the light of the world, and the joy of Heaven.
The mountain still speaks.
May your life echo back.
With love,

—Damiano B. Centola

About the Author

Damiano B. Centola is a prophetic writer, theologian, and poet whose works stir both heart and mind. With a voice that blends biblical clarity, poetic rhythm, and deep spiritual fire, Damiano writes for a generation hungry for truth that both cuts and heals. His books call readers not only to read—but to awaken, to rise, and to return to the mountain where God still speaks.

He is the author of God's Sovereignty: Exploring the Divine Rule Over Creation, History, and Eternity, Divine Encounter: Discovering the Depth and Power of God's Names, I Choose the Call: My Daily Anthem of Devotion, The Lord Is My Shepherd: A Journey Through Psalm 23, The Mother of Corruption: Unveiling Spiritual Corruption from Babylon to Today, and several other works that cross genres—uniting theology, Scripture, beauty, and boldness in one sacred flame.

A messenger of the Kingdom and a servant of the Word, Damiano writes not for applause, but for awakening.

He believes the Sermon on the Mount is not an ancient artifact—it is a present-day manifesto.

He lives with his beloved wife Feebe, whose grace and strength echo through every page he writes.

To connect, learn more, or explore his full library of writings, visit:

www.damianocentola.com

www.ingramcontent.com/pod-product-compliance
Lightning Source LLC
Chambersburg PA
CBHW040109100526
44584CB00029BA/3975